Poetry by the Sea
A Collection...

Tara Chase

1

Poetry by the Sea, First Edition

Published by: Tara Chase

ISBN10: 0977407101

ISBN13: 978-0-9774071-0-1

Manufactured in the United States of America

Preface

This book evolved from a summer of rapture.
Time spent living my life on the small, yet captivating seacoast of
New Hampshire, led me to start my true desire; Writing and
Photography. The selected poems and photos that have made the
"cut" exhibit the true sense of where they come from. Classic
grace and timeless energy are captured forever, enveloped between
these two covers. Life is full of changes, therefore we never stop
learning. The ocean can be a very nurturing teacher. I believe
there are not always answers, sometimes just a feeling. No logic,
nothing easy to analyze. Sometimes we just have to trust our
emotions. This personal philosophy has led me down many
tremendous and stunning memories throughout my life. I have
taken a lesson to mind from each and every one. The beach, writing
and photography are my passions. I cling to them for they bring
me inner peace and much happiness. I breathe them in as if my
last breathe. Taste the salty air and listen to the waves, as you
read about historical towns, calm harbors and view blissful,
picturesque shots of seashores.

This book is dedicated to:

My first masterpiece,
my prince,
my child,

Trent.

Sea of Contents

Ode to the Ocean

Miasma

Gull

Oceanic

Lighthouse

Child of the Sea

Harbour

Isles

Starfish

Vessel

Sonetos

Friend

Lass

Overflow

Mermaid

Ode to the Ocean

When I am weak, you are there to fortify that I am adept in accomplishing anything. When I am strong it is strength drawn from you. Some come with regret, some come with hope. Some constantly to daydream and some to just grow old. Like the tide craves the sands, I am abundantly drawn to you. Drawn by your way to make me surrender myself and I have to say touché! The temple that transforms my heart, nourishing and full of promise, drowning in your arms, collect me up in your merciful skies and keep me from all danger. Feed my hungry soul and provide me with your kindhearted shelter, as my soul lusts on and on. I come to you besieged leaving calmer, realizing the rise and fall of men every day, as I peer out your stretched wings of blue, I am searching for my lullaby. Mesmerized, I am tranquil within. Unconscious I am, as I lye in your sheets of satin sands. You don't know me, but I know you and when my life has dissolved, my spirit will dance upon your shores still!

Miasma

Tiny town, hidden by the marsh, you fill my heart. The times you have seen and the tides that have crashed upon your shores are of such magnitude! O ye of great inspiration to me, I love your splendor and the times past that once lined your hazed streets.

Trying to imagine what they were long ago, I peer aimlessly through your morning miasma. It keeps you hidden, almost as if a secret. I lye in my bed awake at night and listen to the words you whisper, with my windows open anxiously awaiting your knowledge and evening farewell, as your words crash across the street! Many come and many go, but few know your olden times. Few appreciate you for nothing more than your beachfronts, yet, I know otherwise. I know there is more to you. I know the sweet sea-scent you possess, that dashing sense of style you contain.

I drink of your imagination. I press you with a kiss let, realizing your morning rays, crown jeweled and cordial. Friends not foe give and take. I feel as though a transplanted southern gal, yearning for tender rays year round, excepting in exchange, the charm that tiny Rye holds and offers freely while keeping me close. Budding is the dearest and most petite beach rose that hover many of your humble abodes. Rest aside tiny town, you shall always have a friend. Not one who comes only in summer appreciation, but a true friend all seasons end!

Gull

Traveler of the wind, friend to the clouds, I ask you
again...why do I have a drought? You are so free and
I am worn out. I ask you again, what do you see? Can you
tell me my future? Could you sing me a song? I would listen
to your travels all the nights long! Some say you are dirty,
some a bother. I think of you more like a small brother. I am
jealous of your zest for life inland and out. I see you both n
the early morn waking from my beach slumber and when the
lights start to go out. A million men have you seen. You
swoop through the air with great velocity, into the blue skies
you climb only to fall, so low, so quickly, judging them all.
The world stops for no one though, dear brother to me. Do you
always know where you are going? Sometimes you call at me,
as if pleading me to stay! I must leave you for now. Do not
heed my sighs , for I am just a little confused, but will soon
determine all.   I will never disregard you or your eminent and
distinct freedoms which I look to bring forth with a passion,
so true and obvious.

Oceanic

There once was a boy who lived by the sea. He lived in a harbour not far from me. He needed a challenge; he needed a way, so he set sail on an adventure one gloomy day. He was searching hard, but searching for what? Maybe for all that his life was not. Not lack of lust, not lack of luck, but the lack of fulfillment in himself and thereof. He set sail empty and alone; desperately wishing his heart had a home. His tastes were impeccable, his sight so keen, a smile that from China would happily gleam. A hardy laugh, a slow hand, and an outlook on life that was both simple and grand! Many a wave passed under his ship, miles stretched across his long and barren trip. Could he discover his inner most answers? In his head, he must first finish with the dancers. The journey got harsh and the man grew tired. The thoughts he had carried would soon expire. Unsure of what was next to come, he switched course, turned about for to head towards the sun, realizing that each and every single day, questions come as do the answers for which we meditate and pray.

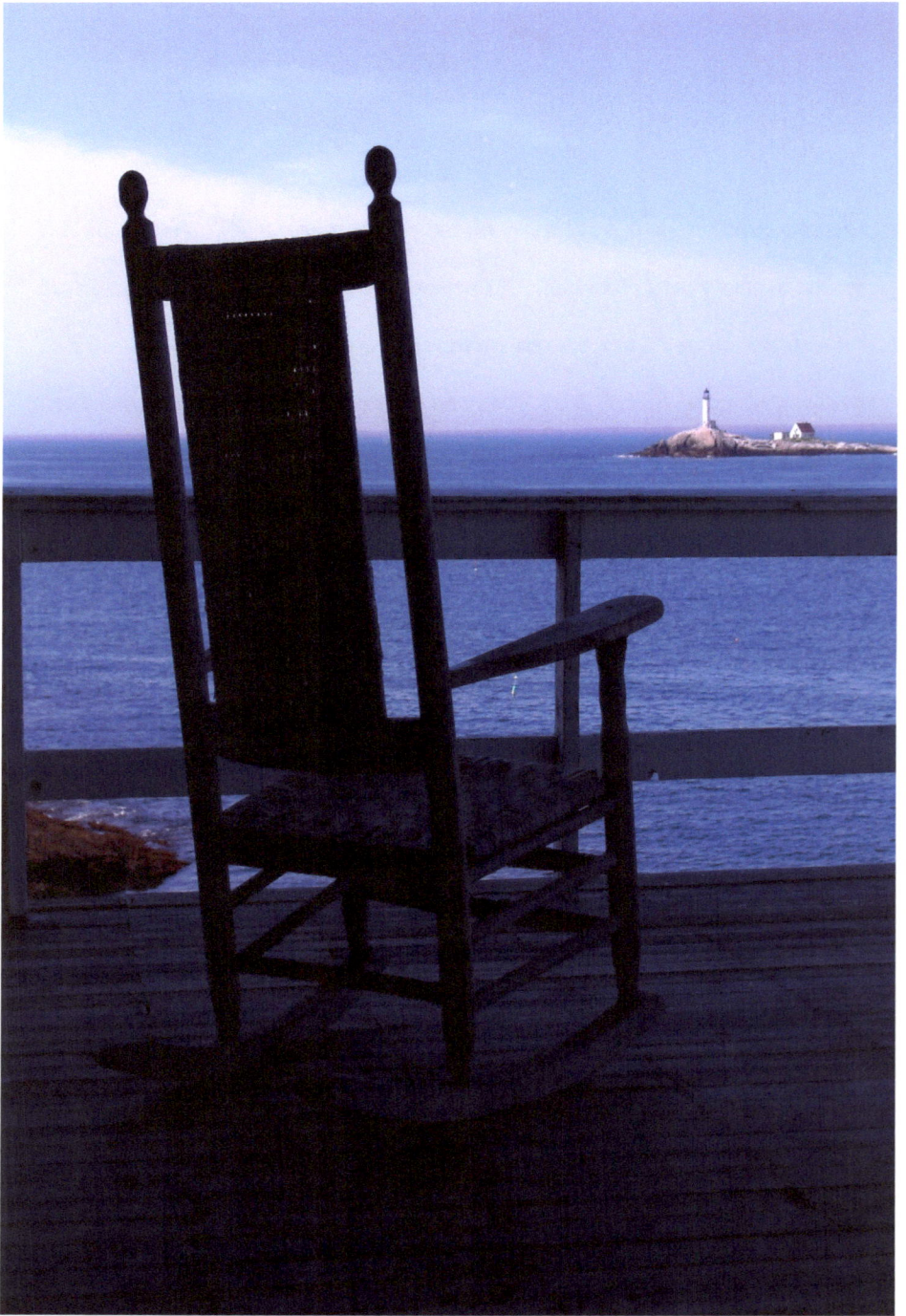

Lighthouse

Innumerable graces, able to save lives, a warm and soft glow emits from your heart. You try time with courage and humbly stand tall. Who amongst your presence could ever fall? Content in waiting for your time of need, by chance some poor sailor will fill that want; hopeful he will change course in seeing your knowledge. You gather audacity staying strong and you endure. Ah, but time is flying, nothing much stays the same, except Thou art fair and surviving! You are a fearless and Godless soldier of the sea, inflexible and unforgiving because you need be. Your affection is not unknown. You prevail o'er the tides! Your responsible reasoning, teaches wisdom of our own great efforts. There are no false doubts, no harmful fallacies; few wounded who have seen your light. Relentless, you are still there, untouched with faith unquestionable, a glory on the sea! Swiftly moving waters and rough winds test your eternal rigidity. Dreams are in your heights and you shall never fall! Great lighthouse, you need not have any walls. Your eyes see many miles and many dreamlike moons...

Child of the Sea

Child of mine own. Child of my blood, thoughts, anticipation, my tears, my anxieties and all my hopes and dreams. You touch the grains individually, with a heartfelt trust for the ocean and her unmistaken timeless energy. Joyful are you, as you run and jump upon her beaches of carefree wisdom. Positive am I, that you will be a part of her always, for like your mother, you love the wind in your hair, the birds flying overhead and the cherry skies that you succumb to as dusk falls. I feel the emotions that you possess while happily dancing in her sands; you've no more a favorite palace!

She is your chateau, vast and endless, with many windows for your little eyes to peek out. I watch the tiny prints you leave next to mine, wondering how many glorious years lye ahead of us. How many moons will we view together during twilight times, as the waves come crashing up to wash away our tribulations? You bring happiness in my life that I never thought I would have. Dreams are becoming fulfilled because of you. I would die to know what dreams you have roaming in that tiny, little mind of yours?

Will you grow up to collect stars? Will you grow up to paint pictures of beautiful seascapes? Will you dance with your mother on her 50th birthday? Will you always bring her seashells? You bring my life the direction needed to stay grounded, always full of surprises; you are my sweet manifestation. I'll always keep you safe from harm my love, next to my minute yet strong body. No tides shall ever separate us. No seas shall ever keep us apart.

You shall always be my child; cheerful, limitless and original, as you will always be the Child of the Sea!

Harbour

Mother of all that is tranquil, peace after the storm, Oh harbour like my mother, to you I feel as if I were born. Vessels stay by your side, like children who adore you and listen to your guide. You teach, harmony, light and life renewed. The lessons are taught and never construed. They are there to be viewed at the start of the day and then again as sundown falls. Busy are you with many feet early in the morn, graciously awaiting the end of the day for the return of all your children unharmed and safe. Serene and calm will your home be til' then, as all your children have set to sea; until such time as they come home to lay their heads fondly upon your breasts. Continually nearby, I call on you daily enjoying all you have to offer; smiling with geniality from inside out, through the lengths of our conversations, the delicacy you hold and the wealth of respect that you earned.

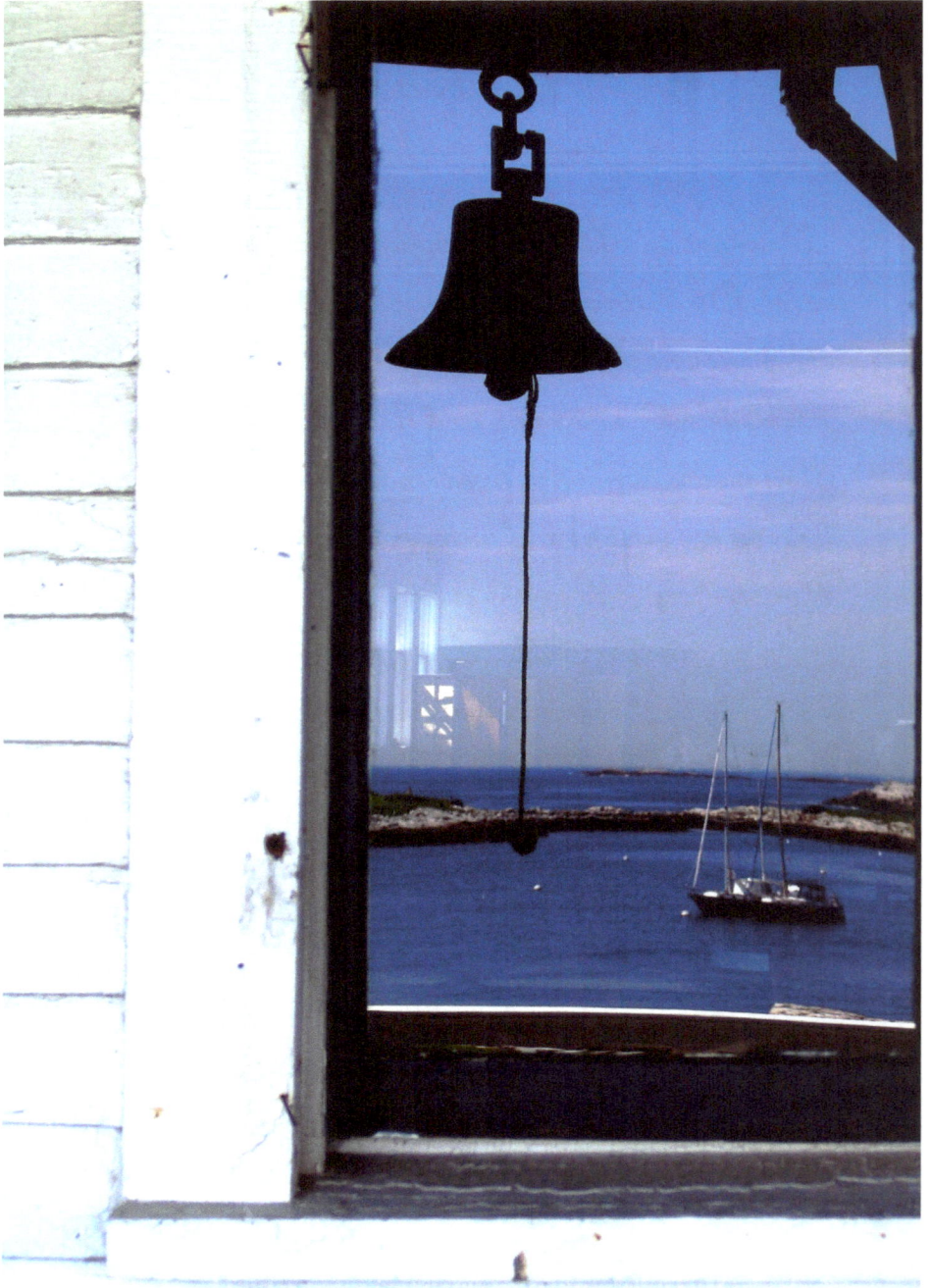

Isles

Their regal nature; the fruitful discovery and fertile lands. The Isles are like that of a treasure, nine to be complete. History has written itself upon her sleeves. Much is buried at her seawalls, a rote unlike one you have ever heard! Love, murder, hardships, silence and life, wish I could have been there when her love was for sale! Alas, I am much too young to remember that precious moment. Yet, I am aware of her years of entertainment and her visitors with such perfections, The Fields, Whittier and of course Mrs. Thaxter. Many artists who would sculpt, artists to paint, tenderly loving gardens, lush with their abundant souls and sailors buried upon her heart. I could have adored those Isles for so many a year! We could rekindle the laughter that once rang on her shores. Children and family, what pray tell is divorce? I would run across the land so strong beneath my feet, grabbing my attention on a clear and visible day. I stand here staring, like she is a Goddess at bay. Tyranny and suspense like seaweed tangled up. Let us shake hands before we must part. Floating and beckoning me to come and visit, fear not for I shall. Obscuring my view temporarily I have lost sight. Ah, but unto mine eyes I find her once again! Shall I come tomorrow dear Isles, to step foot on your noble and rich earth? I am afraid I would never depart. . . .

Starfish

Starfish, Starfish, how can it be
that you live in the water so deeply?
You have five ways which allow you to grow.
It's those five points that make you whole.
A creature of the deep; you live in the sea.
There's nothing you need because you are free!
Decoratively playing in the seaweed,
your magic and beauty intrigue me.
The day brings the Starfish, which sleeps at
night. When the stars return to twinkle their
lights. Upon the days start, so is the Starfish,
bringing old stories of happiness and love.

Vessel

You walk on water, as if a blessed one. Sometimes quiet, though sometimes speaking loudly, wanting to be seen, like a child desiring attention. You are strong and sturdy, a massive power not to be taken lightly. You depart almost before time, so, so early, yearning for your first breathe, heading towards that magical sunbeam miles out to sea! You carry your friends with great confidence. They are in their grandeur waiting to fish with their feet planted firmly upon you. You shimmer and sparkle of barnacles on your sides. A house of worship, you preserve and protect, full up of a wonderfully true spirit! Throughout the day you go steadily along; wave o'er wave, weathering all storms. If the sea becomes angry, you finish your job, not heading in until you have determined time as seen fit. In your long journey, throughout the day, you pick up many treasures; some to be sold, yet some stay, for these are gifts which you bestow for those aboard , who entrust you with your great efforts and your might! They will never lose sight of the thoughts they have taken from that day for a long time to come. Memories of childhood imaginings, family and times of long ago when they were young and innocent.

Soñetos

I'd like a love that knows no boundaries.
I'd like a love that knows no geography.
I'd like a love that is unknown to most.
I want a love that knows no uncertainties.
I want a love that is as deep as the ocean floors.
I want a love that is complete chemistry.
I need a love that is full and ripe.
I need a love that strengthens and encourages me.
I need a love that will never fade.
I deserve a love that is true and open.
I deserve a love that is warm and flowing.
I deserve a love that will love forever.

I lust after the love that dances in my aching heart.
I desire a penetrating love to quench that thirst!

29

Lass

I once was a young lass, strong, friendly, of average
attractiveness. I raised one child from womb to world.
No husband of which I could boast for too long.
Alone, I lived my life, but merry. A friend of mine
the beach was always, with her majestic cerulean skies
like a medley of songs, blending pinks, blues and gold!
Even now as I walk down her path of life, gently she
caresses my feet with her ardent and soft touch. I smile
down upon a young one remembering my own fruits and
how sweet the tastes. I bring to mind that I once was a
young lass, unsure of my journeys end of fruitions and
yea, I walk on steadily, not asking for anyone's hand
in mine, yet planting my feet firmly on the earth.
Memorizing every significant print I make and leave
behind in the sand. Some say a spouse is needed to be
in high spirits and in order to get through life.
I say instead give me the ocean;
I need not be a wife.

Overflow

You are my advocate

You are my peace

You are my trust

You are my laughter

You are my resource

You are my partner

You are my patience

You are my joy

You are my colleague

You are my knowledge

You are my freedom

You are my political party

You are my legislation

You are my organization

You are my company

You are my determination

You are my clarification

You <u>are</u> my friend!

Mermaid

It's so peaceful under the sea but I was here before he left me. The water caresses me now, the way that he used to... to stay in the water, there's nothing I wouldn't do. I'll never gaze upon his face, for he moved to another place. He never did make his choice, so I'll spend the rest of my life not hearing his voice.

I'll remain in the sea. You can try to look, you can try to find me but I only reveal myself to whom I choose. I am the mermaid and I don't owe you.

About the Author

Tara Chase was born in Massachusetts, but raised in Texas where she lived until graduating high school in San Angelo. Tara moved to New England after high school where she would visit her grandparents in the summer when she was younger during school breaks. This is where she came to love the ocean!

She has a son who spends a great deal of time with her at the beach, where they build sandcastles together! Currently, Tara devotes time between Florida and New England enjoying Diving, Sailing, Piano, Running and Biking. She also holds such licenses as: 100ton USCG Master, NH Realtor and Legal Shield.

You may find her at: calltara77@gmail.com

www.ingramcontent.com/pod-product-compliance
Lightning Source LLC
Chambersburg PA
CBHW041803040426

42448CB00001B/23